WICCA FOR BEGINNERS

LEARN WICCA, MAGIC, RITUALS, WITCHCRAFT & BELIEFS WITH THIS EASY-TO-READ GUIDE

FRANK BAWDOE

© Copyright 2021 - All rights reserved.

It is not legal to reproduce, duplicate, or transmit any part of this document through electronic means or in printed format, other than for the use of brief quotations in a book review. Recording, storage, or distribution of this publication is strictly prohibited without written permission from the publisher.

SPECIAL BONUS!

Thank you for adding this book to your Wiccan Library! To learn more, why not join Frank's Wiccan Community and get this additional Free Wicca Starter Kit Book 100% FREE!

Hundreds of others are already enjoying insider access to all of my current and future full-length books, 100% free!

If you want insider access plus this Free Wicca Starter Kit Book, all you have to do is **scan the code below** with your smartphone camera to claim your offer!

CONTENTS

Introduction — vii

1. What is Wicca? — 1
2. The Core Beliefs & The Deities of Wicca — 15
3. The Wiccan Holidays & Festivals of The Wheels of The Year — 23
4. The Overview of Wiccan Covens, Circles, Solitary Practice & the Magic of The Witch — 39
5. Initiation Techniques, Forms of Wicca & Types of Witches — 69

Conclusion — 77
Author's Note — 79
Sources — 81

INTRODUCTION

Wicca is a pagan religion based on nature and practiced with a strict ethical code. It is a modern-day doctrine that honors both a female goddess and a male god, incorporates natural objects and herbalism, and includes the celebration of equinoxes and solstices. Practiced by individuals or covens (group members), Wiccans claim a direct connection to ancient pre-Christian traditions. There is no single Wiccan authority as some are solo witches and some worship in covens. Wicca is someone who believes in the wiccan religion who has knowledge of Pagans and follows their paths provided by Wicca. This book will teach beginners about the history, principles, ethics, philosophy, rituals, and witchcraft of Wicca. Witches maintain the belief that the mind of a human has the power to create change with methods not yet comprehended by science. As part of their ceremonial rituals, spells of healing are performed, as well as honoring their deities. Their code of ethics prohibits any magic harmful to anyone and is only helpful. As a matter of fact, the Wicca religion asserts that negative magic comes back magnified on the perpetrator. Frank Bawdoe introduces Wicca as a present-day gentle and nature-oriented religion committed to God and Goddess and addresses the most important issues of today.

Frank Bawdoe is a devotee of spiritualism and an author who shares a deep-rooted fascination with the philosophy of Wicca and Paganism. Driven by the desire to help the masses embrace spirituality, he aspires to ignite the flames of appreciation in the hearts and minds of readers who are passionate about exploring the essence of life. To explore the realm of paganism and comprehend the depths of Wicca, Frank devotes his time to understanding the principles, philosophies, rituals, and beliefs that define this exceptional modern pagan religion.

Frank Bawdoe has authored numerous books on Wicca and Paganism, including Witchcraft Religion & Spirituality and New Age Divination. An ardent knowledge seeker who proudly walks the path leading to spirituality, he leverages his knowledge to understand the fascinating ways of life. Exploring the depths of paganism with utmost faith and persistence for truth, Frank studies the Wiccan culture, meditation, visualization, magic, and spells to build a better connection with his inner self. Passionate about transforming lives and directing souls, Frank Bawdoe pens down his knowledge to help others get one step closer to spirituality. With his words, he shines a light on the path leading to self-development, happiness, and spirituality. Frank never ceases to miss out on an opportunity to embrace the beauty of life and surrounds himself with nature that scintillates the soul and soothes the mind. He devotes his free time to read, write, meditate, and explore the mysteries of life.

1

WHAT IS WICCA?

WICCA IS A RELIGION DEDICATED TO THE BETTERMENT of mankind and womankind. The word Wicca stems from the word wicce (Anglo-Saxon) meaning to shape or bend nature to your assistance. Based on beliefs in existence long before Christ, Wicca ascertains that Magic is real and exists on the Earth. It pays tribute to the elements and nature and worships two deities, the Moon Goddess and the Horned God. The Moon Goddess and the Horned God represent the feminine and masculine energies of the universe and of nature. It differs from Paganism in that there is more freedom of religion. The God and Goddess simply exist as opposing forces of creation. However, a witch must devote themselves to the Wiccan Rede, "As it harms none, do as thou wilt."

HISTORY OF WICCA

Wicca started in the early twentieth century, developed in England among covens who based their religious practices on the works of writers such as Margaret Murry and other historical Witch-groups. A British born occultist by the name of Gerald Gardner is one of the first and most famous Wiccans. Born in 1884, Gardner was a member of a group of Witches known as the New Forest Coven. Gardner followed the teachings of another Witch by the name of Aleister Crowely and he then went on to be the founder of the modern-day Wicca religion. By the 1950s Gardner's practice spread into Australia, Great Britain, and the United States.

It was Gardner's development of the Wiccan religion that started changing people's perceptions regarding Witchcraft into a more positive direction. Prior to Gardner, Witchcraft was often seen as satanic and barbarous. He also came about in a time where men could be known as Witches. Before this, Witches were usually accused of blasphemy and were almost always female. If a woman stood out for being independent, intelligent, or sexual in nature they were accused of being devil-worshipers because they dared to venture outside of society's expectations of women at the time. The only time men were ever accused of being a Witch is when they were flamboyant or homosexual.

Gardner became familiar with magical practices and occult concepts while he was working in Asia. He studied the work of British occultist Aleister Crowley and other Western literature ideologies of esotericism. Just before the start of World War II, Gardner returned to England and became involved in the British occult community and became the founder of the modern-day Wiccan religion.

Covens usually have approximately 10 members and through a ritual they are initiated. As the members of the coven master their magic practices and learn the Wiccan rituals, they go through up to three degrees. The third degree is for those who want to enter into the priesthood. Following Gardner's system, priestesses are giving priority.

Paganism today refers to those who follow a spiritual journey through life that is rooted in nature, seasonal cycles, and astronomical patterns. Some identify themselves as polytheists in that they honor more than a single god. Wicca is one of the many ethereal paths that fall under the description of Paganism. Asatruar, Druids, Celtic Pagans, and reconstructionists are some of the other types of Paganism. Each branch has its own specific set of traditions, beliefs, and practices. Each branch of Paganism can practice in different ways from each other because there is no universal set of rules or guidelines.

The practice of Magic may have been around since the beginning of civilization, but it has blossomed over the millennia. As the word spread since 1950, the definition of a Wicca has developed into a positive religious practice. It is imperative that even people who are not Witches or practice magic understand what is entailed in being a Witch. It is important to note that the magic practiced by Witches is very natural and not the sensationalized mystery the press often plays up. With the appropriate education, Wicca will become as normalized in society as other accepted religions.

PRINCIPLES OF WICCA

It is customary in most Wiccan covens to have some type of initiation to symbolically represent rebirth, where the newly initiated dedicate themselves to the goddess and god of their choosing. A High Priestess or High Priest of the Third-Degree rank conducts the initiation. It is usually a year and a day of study to advance to the next degree. However, if not a coven member, an individual can choose to a ritual to self-dedicate himself or herself to the Gods of their journey. All followers of the Wicca religion believe in the use of spells and magic, not as a supernatural entity, but as the redirection and harnessing of natural energy to create change. Magic is used as a tool or a skill and can be used by anyone with a bit of practice. Spell crafting tools most commonly used are herbs, candles, athame, crystals, wands, and other special items. Often the magical workings of Witches are performed in a sacred circle with a set of ethical guidelines on why and how the magic should be enacted.

Found in most Wiccan practices are the following core tenets:

- The Divine exists in nature and therefore, nature should be respected and honored. Everything from trees and plants, to animals and rocks are sacred elements. Within the Divine is a goddess and a god to be honored. Since we are all sacred the Divine is present in each one of us, making us all sacred beings worthy of interacting with the god and goddess. Interacting with a Divine entity is not limited just to a select coven or to the priesthood.
- Afterlife and Karma is viewed as a sort of cosmic payback system in that what a person does in their lifetime will be reencountered upon in the next. There is not a belief in the concepts of hell, sin, or heaven.
- Ancestors are to be honored in the Wiccan religion as it is not unusual for Witches to communicate with the spirit world. Many Witches believe their ancestors are by their side at all times.
- Wiccan holidays are centered around the cycle of seasons and the turning of the earth. There are eight

days of power (Sabbats) celebrated along with Esbats on a monthly basis.
- In Wiccan tradition each person is responsible for their own actions. Personal responsibility is a central aspect of the Wicca religion and each member must be willing to accept the good or bad consequences of their behavior.
- Harm no one is a common concept of the Wiccan tradition and means there should be no intentional harm done to another being.
- Non-judgmentalism and without coercion, is the common practice of the Wiccans. Covenants and individual practitioners must find their own spiritual journey and respect the beliefs of others in the process.

TRADITIONS OF WICCA

Wiccans generally accept the concept of an afterlife, and there is a general acceptance of interactions with the spirit world. While not all Witches seek to interact with the dead, many do practice seances and contact with the unknown. Astrology, runes, and tarot divinations are commonly used as methods of communication with other worldly entities.

RULE OF THREE

Some Witches follow the "Rule of Three' also known as the Law of Threefold Return, while others may adhere to the Wiccan Rede. The Law of Threefold Return or the Rule of was designed to encourage a new Witch to think of the consequences of performing any negative magic. Many new Witches are initiated with words of caution from their elders that if they do not honor the Rule of Three when practicing their magic, bad deeds will be revisited upon them three-fold. Some debate the pagan theory of the Rule of Three as a scare tactic to influence new Witches, others say it is only a guideline to keep Witches compliant with the Wiccan code of ethics, and still other covenants swear by it.

It can be an unsettling thought that Witches are going around tossing hexes and curses at people and situations, so the Law of Threefold Return is an effective means for inspiring thought before action. While this law sounds prohibitive, most Wiccans use it as a standard to live by. One may ask, "Why is it called the Rule of *Three*?" It is because three is accepted as a magical number. Pythagoras, the ancient Greek philosopher theorized that the meaning of numbers was very significant. In his eyes the number 3 was thought of as the perfect number signifying the beginning, middle, and end; birth, life, and death; past, present, and future; wisdom, harmony, and understanding; the divine number. It can mean literally three times, or it can mean three times worse. It could also mean that negative actions affect you on three levels: spiritual, emotional, and physical. Another interpretation of those who believe in reincarnation is that the Rule of Three is a cosmic one: what you do in this life will affect you threefold in the next life. Likewise, your life today is a reflection of what you have done in past lives whether they are good deeds or bad. Ultimately, whether you decide to believe in the Law of Threefold Return as a segment in life's little book of instructions, it is up to you to take responsibility for your own behavior and your magic.

TYPES OF WITCHCRAFT

Gardnerian

The Gardnerian tradition appropriately named after Gerald Gardner follows the core ethical guideline of The Wiccan Rede: to do as you like but harm no one. The word rede refers to giving counsel or advice. It is not a rule but a guideline. Gardnerian witches are firmly against any type of coercion and believe in an informed consent. As aforementioned in the Law of Three, thinking before action is a clear expression of free will. This philosophy implies that whatever intentions are placed into this world will be returned thrice multiplied. This concept strongly supports the importance of causing no harm. Gardnerian Wiccans follow these tradition-based instructions that demand thought especially before spell work. Gardnerian Wicca differs from other modern witchcraft practices that focus on the sole practitioner's spiritual development. Gardnerian Wicca is a non-dogmatic religion that allows each initiate to find their own meaning or ritualistic experiences by the use of shared ritual traditions. The focus is on correct practice (orthopraxy) not on correct thinking (orthodoxy) and therefore emphasizes shared practices rather than shared faith.

Alexandrian

Influenced by Gardnerian philosophy, Alex and Maxine Sanders branched off from the Gardnerian coven to start Alexandrian Wicca in the 1960s. The main focus in Alexandrian Wicca are the ceremonies and rites dedicating equal time to the Goddess and God; gender polarity. Alexandrian Wiccans gather in covens during the eight Wiccan Sabbats, full moons, and new moons, and work with ceremonial magic.

Alexandrians emphasize the importance of the wiccan rite of passage, or initiation. Prior to initiation, coven members decide if the person will be a good fit with their coven by interviewing the initiate and through invitations to gatherings and open rituals. An offer to join officially is made and if accepted, the new initiate starts to study without being bound to the vows of the coven. This first phase can last up to a year depending on the member. The potential member is exposed to the close coven bond as well as the elders being exposed to the candidate. Traditionally, the decision is matrifocal, meaning the final decision is made by the high priestess. If welcomed into the coven, the candidate will then have the choice to achieve the first degree of initiation and commit himself or herself to a more serious path. Here the new member must show dedication to the learning and commitment to the craft's knowledge and show great enthusiasm toward learning the ways of the craft. Alexandrian Wiccan tradition believes that all members are priestesses and priests, meaning that every coven member has the ability to participate in a fellowship with the Divine, therefore there are no "lay persons".

Eclectic

Eclectic Wicca is a term given to witchcraft traditions that do not fit into any specified category. It is common for Solitaries to follow an eclectic path, but there are also eclectic covens. An eclectic approach to Wicca utilizes a combination of practices and beliefs from various different traditions and pantheons. Some covens may modify Gardnerian or Alexandrian methods making them different. If a belief or practice cannot be defined, it is termed eclectic. A solo practitioner who is uninitiated may be exercising the craft they have learned from available resources regarding Wicca, but not be bound to the initiation process, and therefore, acknowledges their practice is eclectic. There is some debate as to whether non-lineage covens should be able to refer to themselves as Wiccans, but can be acknowledged as NeoWicca, or non-traditional, new Wiccan. As is customary with all Wiccan traditions there are no insulting or derogatory aspects.

Traditional

Traditional Wicca is usually termed so mainly in the U.S. and applies to groups following Wiccan traditions that originated in England's New Forest region. Traditional Wiccans strictly adhere to Gardner's initiatory lineage and not to NeoWiccanism or eclectic traditions. Traditional Wiccan initiates work with deities who are secret in name as to preserve their sacredness. Traditional Wiccan follows a coven-based practice. Even if there is not a traditional Wiccan coven near your area, you can still find traditional Wiccans who may be willing to share their knowledge and mentor new initiates. As witchcraft continues to evolve with each new generation of witches, varying types of witchcraft will change with the times and with the communities and cultures that practice them. However, traditional Wicca has thrived and survived through changing times and will undoubtedly carry on, even though many don't even realize it is there.

Hereditary

There is no one person biologically born Wiccan, just as there is no one born Muslim, Hindu, or Christian. The Wiccan religion is not orthopraxic, meaning that you believe or act in certain ways that makes you Wiccan. You can indeed be raised by Wiccans, but that does not mean you inherited Wiccan DNA. There are those who have been encouraged to tap into their psychic abilities while growing up, but that does not make them any different biologically or chromosomally. People can inherit family and cultural traditions making them more prone to discover their own spiritual journey in the Wiccan religion. Some claim a hereditary Witch comes from a family that has practiced Witchcraft for hundreds of years and have had the Old Religion passed down over many generations. It is important to note that even when referred to as a hereditary Witch, it may only mean they are third or fourth generation Wiccans.

COMMON MYTHS AND MISCONCEPTIONS

In 1986 Wicca was recognized by the Court of Appeals as a legitimate religion. However, Wiccans are still a generally misunderstood group. Many Witches prefer to be titled Wiccans because of the severe negative connotations associated with the practice of Witchcraft. One very false and negative belief is that Wiccans cast harmful spells. Actually, as aforementioned, it is very much against the Wiccan creed to harm another. Based loosely on paganism's rituals and rites centuries ago, the reverence for the celebrations related to magic, seasons, and the harvest remain the center point of the Wiccan religion. The United States government has deemed Wicca as an official religion, with holidays, varying by state, observed. For instance, eight Wiccan holidays are observed by the New Jersey Department of Education, including Mabon (the beginning of autumn), and allows Wiccan children to be excused from school on those days. Wiccans are entitled to the same rights as any other individual's rights in taking their spiritual path in life.

Another commonly held misconception is that Wiccans are Satan worshipers, when in fact, Wiccans do not even believe in the devil at all. The concepts of heaven and hell have never been a part of the Wiccan religion. They do not believe in only one God, but in goddesses and gods, similar to Hinduism and Buddhism. Likewise, the sacrifice of animals is a misconception of the Wiccan religion. The Wiccan religion is based on nature and Witches have respect for all things living. They may offer a sacrifice to their deities, but they are usually in the form of flowers, bread, wine, or fruit. Wiccans are animal lovers and have a law against any type of blood sacrifice.

There is no Holy Bible that Wiccans follow. They may create a "Book of Shadows (BoS)," or have one passed down from a teacher or family member, but the BoS is only used as a book of reference. Witches also commonly keep a magical diary (grimoire), in which Wiccans keep a record of useful information for practicing their craft, ceremonies, rituals, and spells. Wiccans do cast spells, and the practice of magic is thought to be completely natural. Wiccans believe magic is part of nature and to be used for a variety of good such as healing, prosperity, and personal growth.

Even though Wiccans can be considered somewhat sexually liberal and completely non-judgmental, does that mean they are frequently involved in orgies? Nope! They really do not get involved in the gossip of who is sleeping with who. As long as the adults are consenting, Wiccans do not care if you're gay, straight, transgendered, bisexual, or anything else. Likewise, Witches are not all women. The origin of the Witches legacy is undeniably gendered female but that is because it is a history perpetuated by sexism and misogyny that in the first place demonized Witchcraft and Witches. Witches come in all forms, shapes, and sizes, male, female, transgendered, and of all ethnic origins. Throughout history Witches were persecuted females, while men who practiced magic were revered as sorcerers and magicians. Witches were considered a threat because they did not conform to gender and societal norms which was dangerous in the eyes of a patriarchal hierarchy society.

Contrary to some beliefs, you are not born a Witch. There is always some problematic person insisting they were born a Witch because they come from a magical bloodline. While magical ancestors are a powerful influence, they have nothing to do with whether or not you can be a Witch. Some things are very real in the world of Witchcraft, hexes are real, which is why in part for the Rule of Three, but this rule also applies to positive magic. When it comes to hexes, a commonly used term is black magic. First of all, this can be misconstrued to have racist undertones, while white magic is considered good. Magic is neither evil or good; it is a tool and an avenue for spiritual expression.

You need not have to have years and years of training from confirmed witches before you can cast your first spell and it does not require a full moon, coven, or animal bones to enact them. Casting a spell simply means putting an intention forth and then conducting a ritual to fulfill it, be that mediating, praying, or lighting a candle. For example, let's say each morning you want to awaken with loads of self-confidence. Write an affirmation letter telling yourself how special you are and that you honor the Goddess of beauty and love, Venus, or a deity you feel personally connected to. Simply making a gratitude list and repeating a chant is harnessing that energy and casting a spell.

Witchery is not an expensive practice. With its rise in popularity, witchcraft is now more accessible and the myth that it is evil is becoming debunked. However, here is a heads-up on the Witchcraft industry, many scammers are out there trying to cash in. It isn't necessary to spend a hundred bucks on goop or bags of crystals. Incense, rituals, tarot cards, and candles can help refine your practice. But all that is really needed to practice magic is you. You are more powerful than any items you can buy.

You do not need to be a member of a coven to be a Witch and there are also less governed groups of Witches who practice together in a more casual manner than those covens with highly organized processes of initiation. Others still prefer to be solo Witches. Each person's spiritual journey is very personal, so whether or not to be a member of a coven is up to you.

2

THE CORE BELIEFS & THE DEITIES OF WICCA

WICCANS TODAY HAVE USED THEIR INNOVATIONS TO transform ancient practices of Witchcraft to meet the needs of modern-day spirituality. However, older traditions still offer problems to society and governments worldwide. Educators and scholars of traditional Wiccan still teach the psychosocial realities of witchcraft and the still present dangers of persecution. Contemporary Wicca draws in people who tend to have an empowering nature, giving individuals the ability to shape their own future and giving a voice to those who have commonly been silenced.

While Wicca has much in common with Paganism, modern Wiccan covens celebrate diversity and do not have a single bound set of practices, beliefs, or texts. Some are sticklers for prehistoric philosophies, or they try to revive ancient and indigenous practices as accurately as possible. Wiccans focus on an improved future and see all religions as equal, whereas traditional Paganism accounts for the differences between polytheistic and monotheistic religious practices.

GODS AND GODDESSES

Two major deities are worshiped in the Wicca religion: The Triple Goddess and the Great Horned God. Some Wiccans view these deities as male and female aspects of greatness, and some worship them equally along with other special deities from a variety of pantheons. As previously discussed, many Wiccan Gods and Goddesses are connected to the past with emphasis on healing, protection, love, fertility, and the harvest.

THE TRIPLE GODDESS

The aspects of the Triple Goddess can be connected to several ancient civilizations' beliefs, such as Hera, who has the aspects of Woman, Widow, and Girl. Another example is the Celtic goddess Brigid who had the aspects of smithcraft, healing, and poetry. In the Wiccan religion, the Triple Goddess represents the Mother, Maiden, and the Crone. The Triple Goddess aspects align with the Moon's phases and its cycle of orbits around the earth. These three aspects delineate the cycles in a woman's life of reproducing: premenstrual, childbearing, and menopause. However, a woman literally goes through these cycles in her lifetime, but the aspects also represent male qualities of the human psyche as the circle of life is experienced by all living beings on the Earth.

The Maiden

When the moon is taking its first step toward being full it is known as the crescent-to-waxing phase. When new, the moon is completely invisible until a sliver of illumination appears, this is the aspect of the Maiden's youthfulness. The Maiden is associated with sunrise, dawn, and the season of

Spring; it is a time of spiritual growth. The Maiden accents the fresh potential and newness of life. The qualities of independence, innocence, intelligence, and youth are all associated with the Maiden. Witches may refer to the Greek Goddesses Persephone and Artemis, Rhiannon (Celtic), Freya (Nordic), and other deities. The Maiden is also known to be the first in the series of aspects associated with the Triple Goddess. The Maiden is The Virgin and The Huntress and commonly used in rituals and magic associated with all types of new beginnings, such as new homes, new jobs, and new love.

The Mother

The Maiden transforms into the Mother when the Moon turns full, giving the Earth abundance. The Mother represents Summer's midday, with fields and forests flourishing; a lush time of the year bridled with maturing young animals, nurturing, new responsibilities, and adulthood. Considered to be the most powerful of the three aspects of The Goddess, The Mother Goddess aspects was the inspiration for Gerald Gardner's perception of the divine feminine. At many Wiccan altars, the Mother Goddess is represented by the Roman Goddess Ceres, the Greek Goddesses Selene, and Demeter, and Ceres, the Roman Goddess, as well as others.

The Crone

Referred to as the "Hag" in ancient utterances of the Triple Goddess, the Crone takes over power as the darkness grows and the Moon slowly diminishes. The Crone is the post-childbearing aspect and is associated with the night-time and the sunset. The Crone represents Autumn and Winter and the growing season coming to an end. As the older and wiser aspect of the Triple Goddess, the Crone governs endings; aging-death-rebirth, transformations, past lives, prophecy, visions, and guidance. The Crone has been feared for millennia as a reminder that death is part of the circle of life, just like the dark phase of the Moon comes before the New Moon. The Crone has been slandered because of being misunderstood, probably because of the way many in our society view the elderly. In many cultures the elderly are honored for their wisdom, but in some cultures, the elderly are a reminder of death and sometimes pawned off to healthcare workers as a matter of convenience. The Crone is referred to as The Wise One and has great wisdom to impart. The Crone is Winter, death, and represented by the waning moon and the color black.

THE HORNED GOD

The Horned God is said to travel through the forests as a protector of the Goddesses and all of her children. He is referred to by many other entities such as the God of the hunt, forest, and flock. The God of Life and the God of Death and Resurrection; the hunter and the hunted; the darkness and the light. An ancient wall painting of a man dressed in animal skiing adorned with antlers on its head was first created during the Paleolithic period. He is thought to symbolize a sacred dance by the God to magically increase the number of animals for the hunt. Symbols of the Horned God have been noted in Egypt, Babylonia, and Mesopotamia portraying him as the giver of fertility, Death, and Resurrection. The Horned God's symbol is the Sun, as the Moon is the Goddess's symbol. The Horned God oversees the dark half or the Winter months of the year. At some Wiccan celebrations or rituals, the High Priest will act out the image of the Horned God by wearing a Horned Helmet. Some traditional Witchcraft names for the Horned God include Pan of Arcadia, Dionysus of Greece, Herne, England's the Hunter, and the Celtic name, Cernunnos.

Animal fertility has always been important as is human fertility as a means of survival. But the fertility of the crops is also an important aspect of survival, and for these reasons both The Horned God and The Triple Goddess are fertility deities. As the counterpart to the Triple Goddess, the Horned God grants strength, bravery, male virility, and adventure; he is primal and strong. The Horned God can represent three aspects, like the Triple Goddess, that of the Warrior or Youth, the Father, and the Sage. However, sometimes the Triple Goddess aspects and the two Horned God aspects (night and day) are often mapped as five points of the Pentagram.

ANTI-WITCHERY

Whether it be out of ignorance, intolerance, or confusion, Wiccan are commonly the subject of harassment. The Wiccan religion has even been the subject of child custody cases often arguing against the parental rights of a Wiccan individual. There are some religious elements in the Wiccan religion that lack harmony with Christian teachings. Christians, Muslims, and Jews do not share a belief in Jesus as the son of God, but that does not stop people from having interfaith dialog. This does not seem to be the case with our Wiccan friends. Wiccans have great respect for the spiritual integrity of our planet and lift those elements up for praise. Using the Bible as weaponry and name-calling is deplorable and using Bible passages out of context does not lend itself to the nature of Christianity.

BEGONE HEATHENS

Sometimes those who refer to themselves as Christians use the phrase "Begone Heathens." For some reason they are confused by the differences between Atheism, Paganism, and Heathenism. Those who do not believe in any gods or goddesses are referred to as atheists. A heathen is an individual who applies pre-Christian or ancient Germanic religious practices. Heathens worship the Norse and Germanic goddesses and gods. Heathens believe in a polytheistic philosophy; that each goddess and god are distinct and real individuals not some concept of a greater power. Heathens take their religion seriously, as do Wiccans.

The main difference between Heathenism and Wicca is that Wiccans worship Gods and Goddesses from cultures other than those of the Norse or Germanic. Both Wicca and Heathenism are modern day polytheistic practices that are rotting in pre-Christian philosophy. Both have a feeling of being strongly connected with the earth and all beings that share this world with humans. Both believe they interact with those deities they worship and that the deities are active in all things Earthly.

Wiccans and Heathens do not believe there has to be a special person(s) to contact the Gods for them. In traditional Wicca, everyone is initiated as priest or priestess. Heathens and Wiccans do have some specialized clergy, but they function in the role as teachers or advisers or organizers.

Another primary difference between the two is that Wiccans see their deities as aspects of the Great Goddess and of the Horned God, whereas Heathens see goddesses and gods as separate and unique individuals. There is a greater lack of polarity with Heathenism than in Wicca. Wiccans hold symbolic rituals regarding the union of athame and chalice (God and Goddess). Heathens do not practice this concept. Wiccans are much more centered around magical things with sacred spaces created for the invocation of Gods and Goddesses.

TRANSFORMATIONAL WICCAN SPIRITUAL PRACTICES

The religious landscape for the Wiccan entails a practice of transformation and change. It is an awareness of transformation and the cycles of change in nature and in the life of humans that is central to Wiccan spiritual practices. Witches draw upon their theology regarding the continuous cycles of nature celebrated by the eight seasonal holidays (sabbats) of the solar calendar and the phases of the moon's monthly lunar cycle. Both of these cycles are the foundation for the rituals practiced by Wiccans to celebrate and begin the transformation of the individual and the natural world. Wiccans have an acute awareness of their own creativity in bringing about transformation and change, such as the change of seasons, and devote themselves to the life-long practice of spiritual growth. Healing rituals are practiced as a transformational process from sickness to health.

3

THE WICCAN HOLIDAYS & FESTIVALS OF THE WHEELS OF THE YEAR

WHEEL OF THE YEAR

Symbolizing the eight religious Neo-Paganism and the Wicca religious celebrations, the Wheel of the Year Sabbats include four seasonal festivals which celebrate the changing seasons, and four solar festivals: Winter Solstice, Spring Equinox, Summer Solstice, Fall Equinox. Time was known as cyclical to the ancient Celtics; seasons change, and people came and died, but all was to return again in some form or another and the cycle naturally repeated itself. In present times the Wheel of the Year helps Wiccans to remain balanced in a world which is uncertain. The present-day Wheel of the year was first coined by Jacob Grimm in 1835, a scholarly mythologist, and became fixed by the Wicca movement in the 1950s. The holy days of the Wheel of the Year includes:

Name	Holiday	Earth Event	Date	Occasion
Samhain	Halloween	Fifteen Scorpio	October 31st	Cleaning and releasing. Celebrating the dead.
Yule	Christmas	Winter Solstice Capricorn	December 20-25	Song, fellowship, candlelight, and lighting the sacred fire.
Imbolc	Candlemas	Midway between the Winter Solstice and Spring Equinox: Aquarius	February 1-2	Lunar Fire Festivals Day of Feast and celebration for the recovery of the Earth Goddess after giving birth.
Ostara	Easter	Spring Equinox Aries	March 20-23	Spring cleaning; planting seeds.
Beltane	May Day	Taurus	April 30-May 1	Fertility; Fire celebration. Couples dance around the fire.
Litha	Midsummer	Summer Solstice Gemini	June 20-22	Gratitude for life and light. Honors the Sun God.
Lughnasadh	First Harvest	Halfway between the summer solstice and autumn equinox Leo	August 1	Symbolic gifts of the first fruits given to priests as an offering to deity. Honoring hard work and that it pays off.
Mabon	Thanksgiving	Autumnal equinox Virgo	September 20-23	Time for resting after the hard work of the harvest. A time to reap what was sown. Time to finish up projects.

These eight holy festivals are constructed to bring attention to what each has gained and lost during the year. The Celts and other ancient civilizations believed that being ungrateful was a sin leading the sinner into the pit of darkness, resentment, bitterness, and self-pity. In order to have balance in life people need to take pause and reflect on what they are grateful for and cherish the memory of anything lost.

HALLOWEEN: SAMHAIN

The Sabbats corresponded to the time of year that the natural cycles of the seasons occur. Similar to New Year's Day, Samhain denotes the yearly cycle's beginning. The word Samhain means the end of summer. It marks the end of the Summer (season of light) and the beginning of the season of darkness. Now, darkness here has no negative connotation, does not mean anything evil or sad; there must be darkness to have light, so it is simply part of the human condition. At the Samhain festivals, thanks is given for the past year and reflections are made about loved ones passing on to the other side.

Many of the Samhain rituals resemble the modern-day festivities of Halloween in the United States. This is partly due to the recognition of Samhain being known as a time of 'in-between' where the dead can more easily move into the living realm. It is believed that the loved ones who have passed to the other side can visit during the Samhain, so it is traditional to prepare a feast and leave out goodies for the spirits of the dead. Witches who have wronged someone who has passed do not wear masks so they can be recognized when the spirits of the wronged come back seeking compensation. However, during the Samhain, wearing a mask or disguise was customary as a form of protection against the most potent powers of the spirits, fairies, and dead souls, who traveled at night and could abduct and seduce mortals.

Practices such as bonfires and other 'mischief night' activities are also traced back to Samhain. Paganism asserts that the world began as chaotic and that the divine forces created order. For this reason, it makes sense for Halloween pranks to symbolize this chaos and the rectification of these pranks on the next day shows the restoration of order. Similarly, bonfires symbolize light triumphing over darkness.

CHRISTMAS: YULE

Yule is the celebration of the Winter Solstice when the days start to grow longer. Ancient Pagans saw the Winter Solstice as the birth of the new sun god of the year. Traditionally, trees are considered to be sacred because they are home to spirits and deities. A decorated outdoor tree and gifts are given in honor of the sun god's birth. A bonfire accompanies the decorated tree as a symbol of new beginnings and the rebirth of the light. People gather around the burning Yule log and celebrate by singing songs and throwing a piece of holly into the fire to represent the past year's challenges. Each year a section of the Yule Log is kept to fire up the next year, symbolizing continuity.

Yule also represented the Oak King's triumph over the Holly King who was his brother. These two entities represented the changing seasons. The Oak King governed the earth by conquering the Holly King in the Winter and reins until the mid-summer with the coming of the Summer Solstice where the Holly King returns to battle the Oak King and becomes dominant during Yule. Wiccan tradition holds that the Holly King and the Oak King are dual characteristics of the Horned God. Each twin rules for half of the year. They battle each other to win favor of the Goddess, and then the loser retreats to care for his wounds for six months until he once again will rein the Earth.

CHRISTMAS: IMBOLC

Imbolc occurs at the middle point between the Winter Solstice and the Spring Equinox and is associated with fertility, hope, purification, and pregnancy. Imbolc from Old Irish means "in the belly" of a pregnant sheep. The Imbolc festival symbolizes a promising future and activities involve weaving dolls tributing the Celtic goddess Brigid from corn or wheat stalks to symbolize fertility, luck, and continuity. Brigid, the fertility goddess, looks to an early spring and is celebrated in the United States as Groundhog Day. Some Wiccan covenants change the date from the original February 1st holiday to one which corresponds to the coming of Spring in the area within which they live.

EASTER: OSTARA

Following Imbolc, Ostara celebrates the Spring Equinox. Celebrations for Ostara include many of the same themes as Easter: colored eggs, flowers, rabbits, baby chicks, and fancy feasts. The word Ostara stems from the Germanic goddess of fertility and spring, Eostre, meaning mother of the dawn. According to Wiccan tradition, the goddess comes back from beneath the earth where she lies in sleep for months until it is time to become pregnant with the next sun god born on each Yule. Renewal and rebirth are the emphasis of the Sabbat which is why the symbolization of the egg is important as is the concept of the labyrinth. The labyrinth dates back some 12,000 years ago to the Neolithic Age in areas as diverse as India, Greece, and Ireland. It symbolizes the aspect of dissociating from your own unique external reality in search of a greater meaning within yourself. This is portrayed possibly by the commonly practiced Easter Egg hunt. The ritual of hunting for a hidden egg elevates the person's consciousness to a new threshold.

MAY DAY: BELTANE

With the coming of summer begins the celebration of Beltane. As commonly used in other Wiccan festivals, bonfires play an important role. However, in this instance, the fire represents passion and putting aside inhibitions so one can indulge in their own desires. Beltane, meaning *bright fire*, also celebrates light and fertility. Dancing is an important aspect of the Beltane celebration, often circling around a tree in ancient days. Presently, a Maypole is constructed as a phallic symbol which is adorned with long ribbon strands held by participants as they dance around it. Beltane corresponds with Mayday which is celebrated throughout Europe. As dark days gave rise to increasing light, all of nature, including sprites, fairies, and other unseen entities awakened. During Beltane to ward off fairy spells and other mischievous activities conducted by fairies, pagans would perform cleansing rituals by carrying a lit candle to all four corners of the home, from front to back, and from side to side, connecting eight points of a protective invisible net to symbolize balance and harmony.

SUMMER SOLSTICE/MIDSUMMER: LITHA

Litha is in honor of the Summer Solstice and the longest day of the year. This is the day in June the Holly King defeated his brother the Oak King and the days become shorter. The Litha festival involved feasting on fresh fruits and honey cakes, and dancing. Bonfires are set to protect people from forces unseen. It is a celebration of light over darkness and knowing that in the future darkness will overtake the light. Hence, longer nights and shorter days are only temporary and vice versa. Some people got married on Litha as part of its celebration. It was feared that newly awakened unseen entities were at their strongest by Litha and therefore could do one the most harm. Sun Wheels were made from corn and wheat stalks and rituals were performed for protection.

Witches can be very creative with Litha ritual ideas such as blessing water with magic to passionately grow their gardens and weaving abundance spells under the midsummer's night sky over their gardens. Litha is an inspiring day of brightness and inner power. It is not unusual for Wiccans to nestle into a quiet spot to meditate about the light and dark powers in the world. Some Wiccans follow more traditional rituals of fire, such as bonfire or a small fire in a pot in one's home. Others find Litha a perfect time to practice love magic!

FIRST HARVEST: LUGHNASADH

Lughnasadh is a harvest festival denoting the change from summer to autumn. It is named after the hero-god Lugh and is associated with truth and order. The harvest's first fruits were offered to the goddesses and gods. Lugh was an early Irish deity god of light and whose mother, Tailtiu, died from overworking herself, plowing and preparing the land. Lugh honored his mother's sacrifice by giving a yearly funeral feast which became known as Lughnasadh. Present day Wiccans throw festivities with competitions in archery, horse-racing, fencing matches, and foot races. Lughnasadh also acts as the final celebration before the end of summer.

THANKSGIVING: MABON

Mabon, labeled as recently as the 1970s, celebrates thanksgiving and thoughts about what has been gained and lost over the past year. It is a celebration of the Autumn Equinox. Mabon was named after the Welsh God who was a son of the Earth Mother Goddess. As a symbol of the second harvest, Wiccans may bring seasonal harvests, such as grapes and apples to an altar and then prepare a feast for friends and family. Apples commonly symbolized the second harvest. Rituals are conducted on Mabon to thank the goddesses and gods for a bountiful harvest and to celebrate an equal light day.

On Mabon, day and night are of equal length again; in perfect harmony; light and dark, feminine and masculine, outer and inner, balanced perfectly. But here lies the cusp of change as the beginning of the darkness, once again begins to conquer the light. The night will begin to lengthen and the days to cool and shorten. The trees' sap will head back to their roots, transforming the summer greens into the beautiful golds, yellows, oranges, and the fiery reds of autumn; returning us to the dark from where we came.

Mabon is a time of thanks to the diminishing Sun for the bountiful harvest provided to us. Each turn of the Wheel brings insights and other inner and outer gifts. It is also a time to rest after the hard work of harvest. It is time to finish projects, clear out what is no longer needed or wanted, and prepare for the winter descent and to look forward to aspirations of new hopes and ideas that will be nourished in the dark, awaiting for the return of Spring.

WICCA FIVE ELEMENTS

In the Wicca religion, four elements are associated with means and traits, as well as the directions on the compass in the northern hemisphere. Followers in the southern hemisphere should use the directions corresponding to the opposite. The elements are considered to be the watchtowers, and when casting a sacred circle are invoked for protection.

Air (Increase Psychic Power)

As the element of the east, Air is associated with the breath and soul of life. Air is the element of focus for magic related to wisdom, communication, and the mind. Air whisks away your problems, carries away strife, and transports positivity to those who are far away. Connected to the suite of swords on the tarot card, Air is symbolized by the colors white and yellow. Air is absolutely imperative to our survival, and is an ever-present element which surrounds us, but can't be seen. The sky, birds, mountains, wind, and oceans all represent the element Air. The Air Element is connected to the mind, divination, intellect, and communication.

Similar to the Water Element, the Air Element is about movement; it can easily travel around the world and cause quick changes. Without it we can't breath and the seed cannot be scattered about giving rise to new life. The Air Element also has destructive characteristics in the form of extreme temperatures and storms such as tornadoes and hurricanes. However, when in the form of a mild breeze, the Air Element can be experienced as a calm and gentle whisper of reassurance from the God and Goddess.

Something to consider about the Air Element other than we are constantly breathing is that to truly relate to this iconic element you have to be conscious of your breathing. Therefore, breathing techniques can help you to get the most out of your magical connection with Air. So can taking a nature walk and noticing the feel of the Air moving over your skin. The benefits of fresh air are understated, so making time to spend outside and noticing how the clouds and trees move will satisfy a deeper connection with the Element. Burning incense during rituals involves Air as well as dancing. The direction of the Air can also be used to enhance certain spells.

Fire (Element of Change)

Fire is not necessarily needed for human survival as we did live without it over 100,000 years ago. Fire is possibly the most captivating of the Wiccan Elements, and yet if touched will cause harm to the body. It is an important Element for a comfortable and healthy existence. Fire allows us to cook our meals, keep us warm, and provide light after sunset. The Fire element is associated with illumination, strength, creativity, health, and is represented by the light of the Sun and stars, volcanoes, and deserts. It is constantly in motion while it maintains the health of the forests through cycles of burning and rebirth. The Fire Element demands much respect for anyone who wishes to use it. Fire is the only Element that cannot survive without another material to consume.

Bonfires are often created as part of Wiccan rituals, either by a coven or solo Witch. The sound of the crackling embers and viewing the sparks can bring on a meditative and calm state of mind. Similarly, gazing at the flame of a candle is a way to connect to the Fire Element on a smaller scale. Witches have been known to read the flame of a Fire for signs and visions, described by the way the fire moves and shapeshifts. Some Wiccan rituals use the Fire's ashes for witchcraft, but there are other ways to commune with the Element of Fire. Raising your body heat through dance or exercise or spending time under the Sun are ways to spiritually connect with this classical Element. Fire is represented in leadership, love, energy, and passion. Ritualistically, Fire can be used as magic in baking and for love spells. As it is the Element of transformation, Fire actually represents magic and is the most spiritual and physical of the four Elements.

Fire represents

- Energy
- Inspiration
- Love
- Passion
- Leadership

Water (Absorption, Purification & Wisdom)

As the most important Element for survival, Water is the most essential of the four Elements for without it, everything would die. With the differential gravitational pull of the Moon creating the tides, the Water Element affects all beings considering that 2/3rds of our bodies are water, this shapeshifting element is associated with dreams, psychic abilities, and emotions. Known for traveling the path of least resistance, Water flows easily about the world.

The Water Element takes many forms: ice, gas or steam, and collections after rain only to be reabsorbed by the Sun. It is associated with oceans, rivers, streams, ponds, and lakes, and benefits life with its healing, nourishing, cleansing, and purifying qualities. However, the Water Element is a powerful one and can be life-threatening when manifested in storms, tsunamis, and hurricanes through the interaction with other Elements. It can put out a fire, flood the ground, and corrode seashores and metal. However, in general, the Water Element is soothing to the human spirit.

Swimming in the ocean, lakes, rivers, ponds, and other natural bodies of Water is a wonderful way to connect with the Water Element. Spiritual connections are made by taking the time to reflect upon the way you feel while bathing, exercising, or meditating after your time with this classical Element. Playing in the swimming pool works too, as do baths and showers. Taking the time to honor the Element while you are drinking, taking a walk in a light rain, or just meditating to its sound will fill you with an appreciation for all things in life. Take notice of the many recordings and videos of waves, thunderstorms, and bubbling streams to feel the essence of this Element flowing throughout your life.

Taking a ritual bath before conducting a spell, or celebrating Esbats, and Sabbats will enhance your magical powers.

Water Represents

- Emotions
- Sadness
- Joy
- Intuition
- Going with the flow of life.

Earth (Strength & Wealth)

The ever-present Earth is the foundation of all life. With its versatility and manifestation of both seed and soil and experienced in the eternal cycle of growth, harvest, decomposition, and rebirth, the Earth Element is strength. Earth and its great diverse features found in vases, gardens, valleys, fields, and forests is represented with prosperity and abundance in the form of trees used to build out shelter, and minerals we need to sustain our health. But the Earth Element has the power to destroy life in the form of earthquakes, avalanches, and landslides. The Earth Element has the power to balance our lives and keep us calm during the "peaks and valleys" which life has to offer.

One way to commune with the Earth Element is to appreciate and experience what it has to offer. Hiking, camping, and nature walks are ideal methods for connecting to this classical Element. Simply, taking a stroll through your neighborhood or a park works well too. A fantastic way to experience the grounding and healing energies of the Earth is to simply spend some time in your garden or just by taking your shoes off and feeling the ground. Laying and meditating in the grass or placing your hands up against a tree while taking in how the energy of the Earth can spiritually shift you into a place of stillness and ease. If you do not have a yard or outside area, such as in the case of apartment dwelling, potted plants, herbal gardens, or just using fresh root veggies can do the trick. When using a fresh vegetable, take the time to sense its rawness, smell its essence, and give thanks to the Earth Goddess for its generous bounty. Winter is its season, and its colors are brown, black, yellow, and green. Often before casting a sacred circle, the Earth Element symbol is salt which is used to form the circumference. Soil can be used to clean and connect magical tools or can be added to certain spells.

Earth Represents

- Animal instincts
- Grounding
- Foundation
- Depression
- Vitality

Spirit (Well-being, Joy & Union)

Spirit, sometimes referred to as The Fifth Element, is also called Akasha or Aether. The Spirit Element bridges the gap between the spiritual world and the physical world. While the four classical Elements of Water, Fire, Air, and Earth combined make up the physical world, the Spirit Element exists in each one of them. While the Spirit is not a material, it is present and a part of everything else. It cannot be seen yet is essential for the balance and connectivity of all other Elements. The Spirit is what is summoned in rituals through the invocation of the Goddess and God, and of Earth, Wind, Fire, and Water. By recognizing the Spirit, and having focused and clear intent, this core energy can be used to create change through work with magic. It differs from the other four Elements, in that it is part of all that exists and therefore, does not have a specific ritual or correspondence with magic. Spirit can be associated with the color white and is not connected to any gender, season, direction, or energy type. It is represented by the Wheel of the Year and all magic in its entirety.

The Spirit Element is that of spiritual intelligence, hence it has no specific symbol. However, the pentacle is often thought of when discussing the Spirit Element because of the Star's five points (one for each of the Elements) which is surrounded by a circle which can represent the Spirit holding all of creation together.

In ancient Greek times, where the Western philosophy of the Elements started, it became clear to Aristotle and other philosophers that there was something more to the classical Elements and when it came to the universe, there was more than meets the eye. The term "Aether" was given by the Greek philosophers to the celestial air that the gods breathed. At first, it was thought to be a part of the Air Element but later it was realized to be an entity in its own right. Akasha is an Eastern aspect of the Spirit Element, meaning atmosphere or space. Space meaning not of physical form, present, yet unseen, from which all creation came. Whichever term is applied, the Fifth Element, Spirit, can be challenging to stay aware of in our noisy, busy world within which we live. That is why prayer and meditation, and rituals are important and treasured activities among all types of spiritual seekers. Coming to the altar, calm and still, to observe sacred rituals, it is easier to get back to this intangible and mysterious energy that is all-encompassing. The characteristics of Spirit are represented through ritual, magic, religion, music, art, and writing. It is nowhere and everywhere and unites and connects us to otherworldliness. It guides us past the narrow boundaries of the physical Earth and allows us to be open to something much more vast; going beyond emotion and thought. Even though it is invisible, its presence is greatly felt.

Spirit Represents

- Joy and Union
- Transcendence
- Transformation
- Change
- Everywhere and Nowhere
- Within and Without
- Immanence.

4

THE OVERVIEW OF WICCAN COVENS, CIRCLES, SOLITARY PRACTICE & THE MAGIC OF THE WITCH

A BASIC COVEN IS A GATHERING OF A GROUP OF initiated Witches. Each coven member specializes in a specific branch of magic, such as the harvest, healing, and love. According to the U.S. Census Bureau, Statistical Abstract of the United States (2011), approximately 1.5 million individuals, identify as Wicca. After studying the Wiccan religion for a year and a day, initiation puts the new Witch on the road to making things official. By joining a coven, the new Witch has the chance to become a high priest or high priestess, leading those with enough education, dedication, and experience to become a Wiccan coven leader. Coven meetings generally involve sabbats to celebrate the Wheel of the Year festivals, and esbats, which are non-sabbat meetings such as phases of the moon. The full moon appears once a month and lights up the sky, presenting a time for Wiccans to pay tribute to the Goddess. Esbats are thought to be the "second" Wheel of the Year and are the counterparts to seasonal changes known as Sabbats. Both Sabbats and Esbats focus the ritual on God and Goddess contributions to the circle of life found on Earth. During an Esbat, covens commune to hold rituals focusing on the Moon's relationship with the Triple Goddess. The Witches create magic under the Goddess's divine light. Solo-Witches also observe Esbats along with Wiccan all around the world who are worshiping the same celestial event.

Esbats and Sabbats celebrations vary greatly from coven to coven, Witch to Witch, and tradition to tradition. But the Goddess is always up front and center, in the form of one of her many aspects. When the moon is full and it is Springtime, Wiccans may focus the Esbat to honor the Maiden, during the Autumn and Winter, the Crone. Sometimes, covens may have a specific magical spell during the Full Moon ritual and choose a Goddess that is aligned with that goal, such as Aphrodite may be invoked for spells related to abundance. Ritual magic is often practiced at Esbats and sometimes they are the main event. Covens might be working to benefit one or more of their group members, for the community as a whole, or even for the whole world. Solo-Witches may work spells at the Full Moon ritual for more personal aspirations, or to cast bigger intentions for healing the environment or peace in the world. In general, magic at a Full Moon celebration is used to bring about positivity, joy, love, prosperity, and spiritual and physical wellbeing.

THE CIRCLE

Both man-made and natural describes the space utilized for Wiccan rituals. This is a good description because it evokes the spirituality that lies somewhere in between. The Wiccan Circle of magic ideally occurs in a naturalistic setting but can also happen indoors. It needs to be a sacred space that accommodates all members and provides a certain level of privacy. Witches unmake the sacred circle when the ritual is over even when it takes place outside. The Circle exists temporally for the duration of the ritual. While the Circle is in existence, it is dedicated to a specific rite, the ritual is then performed, and then the Circle is dismantled. A perfectly normal dining room may be temporarily transformed into a sacred place of worship, then once again returned to a typical dining room. No Circle is ever exactly the same. Witches may create the Circle ritual in the same place with the same casting many times, yet each casting ritual is completely unique. Quite interestingly, a Circle can be cast just about anywhere. The space within is considered to be a place between the Natural, realms of deities, and Human world. It is not of this world or otherworldly, it is a place fit for entrance of the Gods and a sacred place for the Gods and Goddesses to communicate with their followers.

By no means do Wiccans believe they are transported to another world, but the outer edges of the Circle mark the line between worlds that mandate different parts of the Witch's personality (Craft personality) and require different actions. When a Wiccan crosses the circumference of the Circle and steps inside, it is said that they leave their worries and fears behind and turn their attention to the deeds to be done within the Circle. The Witch is transformed into his or her sacred role which is acknowledged by using a Craft while in the Circle. In some respects it is like the Witch's magical personality is revealed and all that that is authentic and sacred has been transformed from the mundane to the spiritual and back again every time a Circle is cast. Confidentiality about Wiccans, Witchcraft, and rituals is of authority by oath. After breaking the circle, a Witch is to leave the details and the identities of the members in confidence, as such the identities, exact wording, and specific details regarding ritualistic gestures will not be disclosed. However, the rituals discussed will be close in structure and in spirit to those experienced.

STEP BY STEP INSTRUCTION ON HOW TO CAST A CIRCLE

- Step One: Using your mind, incense, or a broom to clean your space. Mentally you can push out, you can burn away with incense, or sweep away with a broom.
- Step Two: After you have figured out how you want to clean you are ready to define your sacred circle. Consider your location and space carefully. It can be as small or large as you wish. You can mentally define your circle or use crystals or candles to mark the elements or directions. Use a cross pattern if mark The Earth, The Wind, Fire, and Water Elements or a pentacle for the Five Elements which include the Spirit.
- Step Three: Begin by facing the east if casting a circle to call upon the elements. As you move clockwise, you will end up facing North where you can start your spell or ritual work.
- Step Four: While standing in your circle focus on your breathing and begin to relax; take all of the time necessary to feel centered, present, and calm.
- Step Five: Start to envision the Element, such as with Wind, that it is circling around you while saying "I call on you, Element of Air."
- Step Six: Start moving clockwise toward the south and picture the flames crackling around you and the

Sun's warming presence: "I call upon you, Element of Fire."
- Step Seven: Start turning to the West picturing waterfalls, waves, streams; water flowing around your being "I call upon you, Element of Water."
- Step Eight: Start turning to the North, imagining the Earth's fresh scent after a rainfall and how the cool soil feels under your feet. Envision the darkness of a cavern and the silence: "I call upon you Element of Earth."
- Step Nine: While facing North, imagine your feet sending columns of light down deep into the Earth's core. Pull this energy to you from the Earth's center; into your being and picture a flowing white light, making the circle: "Under the Spirit, with these Elements, I cast protection circle within, below, and above." Here now you enact your meditations, spells, and rituals.

CIRCLE TIPS

If you need to leave your circle temporarily before the entire process, hold a wand or dagger by hand and create a cutting motion across the boundary of the circle: "I use this wand to open a door." Your wand will direct your energy to open a path. When you come back just do the same process in reverse to close the opening.

OPENING/CLOSING A CIRCLE

Facing the North, start the process with "Thank you Earth for your energy; Farewell. Opening or closing a circle is a method for thanking the Elements for helping you to release the energy you have built. Next facing West to release Water: "Thank you for your energy, Water; farewell." Turning to the South: "Thank you for your energy, Fire; farewell" and then face the East and release Air: "Thank you for your energy, Air; farewell." Ending with facing the North to release Spirit: "I bid you farewell, Spirit. I open this circle and send back into the ground the energy.

RUNES

Those seeking advice can turn to an oracle. The term rune means mystery. It is a system of reading utilized to gain insight or answers to questions or situations. Usually, runes are made of stone with a runic alphabet symbol inscribed on them. Elder Futhark is one of the oldest types of alphabets symbolized on runes. It features 24 runes, the first six spell out "futhark". The Old English or Anglo-Saxon version of runes were adapted making up the Anglo-Saxon Futhorc alphabet. Each rune symbolizes a letter of the alphabet and also has symbolic meanings. While very relevant today, many of the rune symbols are rooted in traditional meanings.

An example: Elder Futhark:

- F, Fehu: wealth and/or domestic cattle
- U, Uruz: wild ox.
- T, Thurisaz: a giant or thorn
- H, Hagalaz: hail or frozen pellets of water
- A, Ansuz: ancestral god
- R, Raidho: chariot or wagon
- K, Kenaz: torch or beacon

The Origin of Runes stems from an alphabet that was utilized by the Nordic and Germanic tribes of Scandinavia, Britain, and northern Europe for magical, writing, and divination purposes. Runic symbols have been found on weapons, stones, jewelry, and other objects dating back to the 3rd century AD, and probably were here long before that. The runes can assist you during problematic times and predict what is most likely to happen. They do not give exact answers or act as a type of fortune-telling, and they do not offer you advice. They do, however, offer suggestions on how to handle different variables if a situation does in fact occur. Runes offer simple hints towards answering your questions but leave it up to you to use your intuition and to work out the details. Readers of Runes know that the future isn't set in stone and each of us has the power to make our own decisions and follow our own unique path. Therefore, if there is uncertainty or you are uncomfortable with a reading, the power is within you to change your path. Runes can be used on many different occasions, especially in situations where you see an incomplete picture, or you have insufficient information.

Remember casing runes is not fortune-telling. Focus your unconscious and conscious minds on an issue that you are asking the questions about. This way, when casting the runes, they are subconscious choices that have been made, they do not fall randomly. Keep your questions or issues clearly in your mind when you cast your runes. Remember casing runes if for taking a look at potential causes and effects as well as noting their possible outcomes. You can make your runes out of stone, bones, crystals, wood, or metal; a simple set is all that is necessary. However, after practicing for a while and if you have developed a passion, then it is wonderful to buy or make a special set. There are many to choose from, so put your creative cap on and choose what you are drawn to such as carved stones or crystals. Whichever you choose, it's up to you; it is how you use them that matters. Most rune sets come with instructions telling you what each represents by its symbol and how to interpret them.

Runes are usually kept in small pouches with drawstrings to keep them together and clean or you can keep them in a decorated box. You would not want to lose one by accident. Make sure to have a rune cloth handy. It should be white and small so you can see the runes on them when reading. The cloth acts as a boundary for casting your runes and keeps them free of dirt or damage. It takes time to learn how to master the craft of rune reading. There are many guides, books, and online resources out there to help you to fathom runic meanings and the role they play in your life, and to the issues and questions you may want to explore. It is very helpful to be willing and open to using your intuition in revealing what the stones have to say. It is normal to at first not be sure. Write down your thoughts about any runes and see if their meanings come to you over time. If you cast a rune and it falls upside down on your cloth, that means there is a reverse or alternative definition. Even the most experienced rune casters can be unsure about a specific rune meaning but it suddenly comes to them at a later date. Some sets of runes have a blank one. But opinions vary widely on their validity. Traditionalists believe that there is no evidence historically that blank runes were ever used. It is up to the reader of the runes on how to proceed with a blank rune. You can include them or exclude them if that is what you are feeling at the time.

When it comes to reading your runes, start out in a quiet place, clearing your mind to focus on what you are about to read. Meditated on the question or issues and pray or call upon the spirits or elements to guide you. Have your rune cloth ready. There are many ways to cast your runes, similar to laying out tarot cards. However, on your first try, start by choosing one rune and accessing its significance. Once you are content with your progress, then move toward analyzing your casts and layouts.

- The Three Rune Layout: Ideal for starters. Randomly pick three runes and place them on your cloth. Rune number one should be placed on the right, with number two in the middle, and number three on the left (3,2,1, order). Rune number 1 symbolizes an overview of your question or issue. Rune number two (the middle one) symbolizes a challenge. Rune number three symbolizes a potential course of action that you can take.
- The Five Rune Layout: One at a time, select five runes and place them on your cloth in the following pattern: Number one goes in the middle, with the rest forming the shape of a cross around it. Place number two to the West (left) of the middle rune; number three to the north (top); rune number four to the south (bottom); and rune number five to the east (right). You can either place them face up and turn them over one at a time to read or conduct a straightaway face up reading. In this pattern, the three runes in position 2-5-1 (horizontal) symbolize your past, present and future. Ruin four (below the middle rune) identify what areas of the issue or the problem you are seeking answers to need to be accepted, and rune three (to the right of the middle rune) identifies what assistance you can receive that is related to your issue or problem.
- The Nine Rune Cast: If you are trying to see where you are positioned in your spiritual journey and what is to come next, the magical number nine,

according to Norse mythology, is the cast you can use to put to use your intuition. For the Nine Rune Cast, meditate on your spiritual wishes, and pick nine runes, randomly. Hold them in your hand for a minute or two and then scatter them around on your rune cloth. It is thought that the rune in the middle relates most to your current issues, situations, or questions. Those scattered around the edges are not as important. If the runes are touching, they may have influences that complement each other, but if they are on opposite sides, they may symbolize influences which are opposing. Focus your attention first on the runes that fell face up: jot them for reflection later. Then turn around the runes that fell upside down; keeping them in their same position, read them. These runes may symbolize future possibilities or outside influences.

GROUNDING

Earthing or Grounding power is a way to be personally connected to the energy of the Earth. When feeling anxious or stressed, grounding techniques are a great way to release any overloaded energy from within yourself. And, if you need energy, grounding techniques enable you to pull it from the Earth providing you with enough power while not exhausting your own supply. To begin, sit comfortably with your hands flat on the ground or lay flat on the ground. Breathe deeply three times while picturing energy flowing through you into the Earth or do the opposite if you are needing the energy. Keep visualizing the flow of the energy until to get the desired effect. Another technique is to envision yourself as a tree, deeply rooted into the ground, feeling the flowing energy through your spine.

CENTERING

Once feeling grounded, you may consider centering your energy. The center of your physical body is also your place of balance, your center of gravity. This place lies somewhere between your navel and your breastbone. You may also know if you have an energy center where you store your personal energy. If you need to locate it, picture something you love with great emotion, when you feel the emotion swell, pinpoint its area in your body; this is your center. Begin by putting yourself in the same position you used for grounding, and relax your physical, mental, and emotional awareness at the center of your body.

SHIELDING

To protect yourself from dangerous, depleting, or counter-productive energy, use the shielding technique; it's easy. Create a sphere or clear bubble of light surrounding your body. Imagine how it moves with you and protects you. Picture it as an actual shield and with great practice you can learn how to shield your home, car, or even your bed.

VISUALIZING

The ability to visualize something in your mind allows you to create a complete mental image of an event, person, place, or thing. You can visualize sounds, tastes, sights, and create tactile sensations in your mind. It is like experiencing your senses when you dream, only you are not asleep. Visualizing something in your mind makes it much more accessible. For instance, if you can see yourself as a successful writer, you are more likely to become one. Here are the steps for how to visualize:

1. Think about a time when you were content or happy.
2. With your eyes closed, breathe deeply.
3. Visualizer yourself at that happy time. Try to remember the scene, smell, sounds, tastes, and feelings.
4. Practice visualization right before you go to sleep and just after you wake up as these times enhance your ability to connect to your unconsciousness.

MEDITATING

Practicing meditation helps you to silence the busy chatter in your mind and access profound spiritualism and relaxation. There are numerous benefits to mediation, physically, emotionally, mentally, and spiritually. It can relieve pain and reduce stress, helping you to access your magical skills easier. Use mediation to increase your insight on how to communicate with Goddess and God, the Elements, and your inner Witch. Witches use meditation to clear their thinking and ready themselves for magic, ritual, and divination. There are two ways to meditate, concentration on a single mantra, your own breathing, or on a single image and mindful meditation which means being attuned with all and everything sacred. You can train your brain to recognize each and every thought, sense, and perception that passes through you with getting held up on a single one. Here is one way to use concentration meditation:

1. Wearing comfortable clothing, lay or sit comfortably with eyes closed.
2. Focus on your breathing, feeling the sensation of the air moving in and out.
3. Every time you begin to feel distracted, calmly redirect your thoughts without judging yourself for getting distracted.
4. Note: You can also use words, prayers, sounds, or whispers repetitively.

RELAXING

It is well known that anxiety and stress obstruct the flow of positive energy and take a terrible toll on your spiritual, physical, mental, and emotional health. They deteriorate the quality of life. Wiccans practice relaxation techniques to prepare for ritual as it helps to concentrate and focus on the task at hand. Again, breathing exercises come in handy for relaxing. Also, a good dose of muscle relaxation therapy will help take the tension out of a stressed-out body. While breathing in your nose and out of your mouth; deep breaths, concentrate on each muscle group or body part starting with your feet, moving up to your ankles, then your legs, abdomen, chest, arms, neck, and head. Do this for thirty minutes each day and you will notice a difference.

EXERCISING

Exercise can be a celebration of magic. Magic is carried out with the hope flourishing, not feeling small or shrunken. Witches can use exercise to deeply and physically connect with Spirit. It is a way for the body and magic to dance together in a sacred rhythm. It is a way to love your body and workout both your physical and spiritual fitness. Exercise, both physical and spiritual, enhances the quality of life. Rewarding magic and effective ritual takes concentration and stamina. If you are in good health, you can achieve a much more fulfilling practice in spiritual fitness. Yoga, aerobic exercises help you to manage your stress and protect you from becoming depressed and other emotional problems. Of course, you should check with an MD to develop the best exercise plan that fits your lifestyle, age, and any medical conditions.

One way to "get your magic on" is through what you wear when exercising. Wearing clothes you enjoy putting on that make you feel comfortable, will remove one distraction and make it easier to concentrate on your activity. Workout wear can be realized as ritual attire since you are dressing for an occasion, a ritual. This means choosing your magical colors. Maybe bright yellow gym clothes inspire your positivity, or black and red may draw upon your inner strength. Designs can be part of your ritual as well. As you progress in developing the best version of yourself, you may want to add to your ritual toolbox. Maybe adding gloves for your workout or special gym shoes. Nike gives some practitioners an added "swoosh" of magical incentive. Afterall, Nike was the winged victory Goddess. Clothes may want to listen to inspirational music while wearing earbuds as the sounds help them to delve more deeply into their ritual. Don't forget your water! There is magic in holding the cup or bottle and pouring energy, intent, and gratitude into the water. The gratitude is for its nourishment and cleansing attributes. Entering and leaving a sacred space in your exercise area is a way to open and close your ritual. This is the activity that begins the magical practice and defines the moment it ceases. All that matters is doing it with intent.

LIVING AND WELLNESS

Using the weekends to catch up on your sleep, means you are not getting enough of it. We have heard the saying "Don't underestimate a good night's sleep." Well, it's true. Not getting enough sleep hinders your concentration and focus and makes magical gratification more difficult to achieve. It also impairs your ability to drive safely and impairs your memory. It is impossible to maintain healthy spiritual and physical wellness without eating right. All of the practice in the world will not lead to success without proper nutrition. To the Wiccan, food is symbolic. With magic and ritual intentions for strength, love, healing, and prosperity can be achieved. This is the reason for food being consumed as sacred, therefore it is sacred in its preparation. Consider the following when preparing food:

- In figuring out which ingredients and preparations to be used, make sure to first construct your intention.
- Find out if there are mantras that will help you for your specific intentions.
- Keep your kitchen or cooking area spiritually and physically clean. You can use incense rituals.
- Chop your ingredients into symbols or magical shapes.
- Always stir corresponding to the sun's movement (clockwise).
- Concentrate on your intent in meal preparation. This will infuse into your food, positive energy.
- Strength and personal development can often be found with Wiccans who serve the community.

Witches believe, in general, that all is connected and come from and are integrated with Divine energy. The circle of life is connected by an energy manifested from Divination. Wiccan service is based on a shared belief in preserving the Earth's resources, ending poverty, preserving indigenous cultures, protecting nature and its animals, encouraging education and the arts, advocating for freedom of religion, practicing conflict resolution, and laughing. Laughing is therapeutic. It releases the natural antidepressants in the brain and elevates your mood. It is a spiritual way of celebrating joy, bliss, and delight.

HOW TO CONDUCT A NATURE RITUAL

1. Find a special place in Nature where you can meditate. The forest, by a lake, in a meadow, near the ocean, by a mountain, in a cave are all places to connect with the Elements and can be away from the company of humans.
2. Sit calmly noticing your surroundings and start to shift your focus from human centered to Nature awareness.
3. While meditating be reminded that you are a part of Nature and that you are there for Spiritual nutrition and to strengthen your connection to Nature.
4. Envision yourself being lovingly held by Mother Nature, as you feel the gentle Air caressing you as the Sky and Earth provide you with spiritual energy.
5. Express your thankfulness for the Cosmos, the Planet, and the Elements for their nurturance to all lifeforms.
6. Notice the life in all of the plants surrounding you

and focus on just one of them. Touch, smell, and if you can taste it essence; essentially become the plant or one with the plant.
7. Return yourself to your human form and thank the plant for being a friend, a relative, a teacher.
8. Reflect on your spiritual time as a plant.
9. Next do the same with the environment surrounding that same plant and experience being part of nature.
10. Notice the sound of the Wind, birds, and animals.
11. Notice the colors, patterns, rhythms, and directions.
12. Take a mental picture of your spiritual sanctuary so you can visit it anytime while meditating.

PLANT MAGIC

Wiccans honor wild things and use materials provided by the Earth for their spells and rituals. In this way, they honor the Spirit Element. Plants have been around much longer than humans. It is safe to say that plants and herbs are part of the oldest known magical instruments. Prior to separating magic from medicine, healing was treated with herbal concoctions, ritual, and prayer. In present times, a simple cup of herbal tea can have a spiritual and emotional, as well as nutritional benefits. Plants symbolize the magical powers of the Elements. They start as seeds in the Earth, where they are nourished by the minerals and interact with sunlight or Fire Element. This in turn converts carbon dioxide into oxygen directly involving the Element of Air. Air in the form of wind and breezes gives way to more plant life with their stems and leaves which then scatters seeds to continue the cycle of life. All of which cannot occur without the Element Water. Plants are crucial in regulating the water cycles on Earth through purification and aiding the soils movement into the atmosphere. That is a perfect illustration of how Fire, Earth, Water, and Air are connected to the magical essence of plants. Plants can sense their surroundings and even communicate with other plants. Plant intelligence is the subject of much study these days. In natural and unnatural settings plants cooperate and communicate through their underground system of fungi and roots. They help one another by exchanging minerals and other nutrients and warn each other of impending dangers.

The science behind plant intelligence is a beautiful illustration of the wit inherent to Mother Earth. Wiccans tap into the magical energy of plants when incorporating herbs into their spells. That said, working with a garden is a great way to commune with Mother Earth. Growing your own flowers, berries, and herbs keep you in touch with the wind, rain, sun, and water, not to mention the role that animals and insects play in both life and death to continue the circle of life. When it comes to practicing magic, herbs are very useful and versatile. You can keep them in spell jars, sachets, and other charms used for your magical crafts.

ASH

Ashes symbolize transformation, change, and the union of Earth, Wind, Fire, and Water. Ash represents rebirth and strength. One of the great aspects of ash is that you can create it with endless combinations of ingredients. As with any material used in magic, holding it, wearing it in the form of jewelry, or sprinkling some on your altar will hold your spirited intentions. When gathering for Fire rituals to honor deities, offerings are ash can be handed out to each participant to tie everyone together during the celebration. Ash can be used for ointments, potions, and magical ink with which to pen in your Book of Shadows. Creating combinations of ingredients when sourcing your ash should have an inspirational meaning to you. It can be as simple as utilizing the ashes left from burning your incense or choosing your favorite smelling bark or wood with which to make ash. When creating your magic ash, consider your intent and what will enhance your ritual leading to more spiritual growth. Take care not to burn anything toxic to you or the environment. These items will be magically weak anyway. You can place under your pillow dried leaves turned to ash to stimulate prophetic dreams. Scatter the ash in all four corners of a room for protection. Wiccans commonly keep ash in a sachet to ward off negative energy. Carry it with you when you travel for safety.

BIRCH

The Birch tree, also referred to as the "White Lady of the Woods" is a symbol of great beauty and strength. Since it is one of the first trees in the spring to sprout new leaves, it has long been associated with rebirth. Considered to be a species of pioneers, Birch trees are the first to recuperate from fire burned land. Hence, there is a traditional association with new beginnings and fertility. In magical practice Birch is thought to inspire fertility, inception, and purification. It has antiseptic properties and is traditionally utilized for making the Witch's broom. The Birch spirit is said to offer protection and courage for those who may step outside of the safe and normal. Strips of Birch or Birch paper (so to speak) is a valuable tool used in witchcraft, so make sure if you buy it in a store that it is not an imitation. Birch has the fresh aspects of the Maiden, the Mother's generosity, and the wisdom of the Crone. It provides an abundance of positive energy and potency to magic. Use to meditate upon when starting a new project or invoke its spirit during any hardships for resilience.

You can pen your wishes onto paper made from Birch bark and then burn it to make them come true. Carry a piece of Birch in your pocket to protect you against fairy tricks and hexes. Use your Birch handled besom to sweep out dust and dirt from your home, so blessings can cascade in and your home can be purified. Putting up a piece of Birch tree over or near your front door will stop ill-wishes from entering. Make your magic wand from a piece of Birch for inspirational and protective spells.

CEDAR

Among some indigenous people and Wiccans Cedar is considered a sacred part of religious ceremony. The branches and leaves are steeped in tea or burned as incense to ready ritual space. Wiccans believe that Cedar creates harmony in emotions and prepares the mind for meditation. Cedar has medicinal purposes in that it functions as a disinfectant, lowers fevers, and calms a cold or flu. Because its wood doesn't decay it is considered too sacred to use as fuel for fire. Cedar is associated with longevity, growth, and power. It is used in making coffins because it doesn't dampen or decay and it repels insects. It is considered to be a psychic boost and when burned can attract money.

ELDER

The Lady Elkhorn or Elder tree symbolizes birth and death as well as beginnings and endings. The Elder tree is associated with the Crone as its magic gives advice on what to start and what to cast away. Elder has many benefits and medicinal purposes. It can be used as a pain and inflammation reliever and it is full of vitamin C. Making tea with its flowers can alleviate sore throats, help a cough, and help you to become regular. It is also great for kitchen witchery to be used magically in jams, syrups, and wines.

HAWTHORN

The hawthorn tree is known to Wiccans as a cleanser of negativity from the heart and inspires forgiveness and love. It represents the oppression of paganism and their celebrations by the Christian Church. The Hawthorn three is revered as the "tree of enchantment" and well protected by faeries. Its lovely flowers are thought to help prayers to reach the Goddesses and Gods. Folktales have it that if you, on May 1, are sitting under a Hawthorn tree, there is a good chance of being carried away to do good for the faerie world. Witches use the hawthorn blooms in spells for good luck while fishing, fertility, and happiness. Powerful wands are constructed from the Hawthorn tree and its blossoms are thought to be an aphrodisiac. Therefore, it is perfect for marriage and love spells. May Poles were originally constructed from Hawthorn trees. The magic of the Hawthorn wards of evil and Wiccans light candles on the Hawthorn tree at dusk on eve of May Day to welcome the coming of Summer. Having medicinal characteristics, the Hawthorn tree offers many remedies and brings happiness. However, caution is advised because of the Hawthorns--thorns! It is thought that the thorny crown worn by Jesus Christ was made from the twigs of the Hawthorn.

MAPLE

Maple trees symbolize love, longevity, promise, and the wisdom of balance. It is known for its magical sap or sugar which represents abundance and success. This may be due to Native Americans using Maple sugar for trade. It has both masculine and feminine energy. Its planetary associations are with Jupiter and the Moon and it is sacred to Virgos and Libras. The sacred bird of the Maple tree is the great horned owl. Many Witches use wands made of Maple for spiritual work. It is also considered the wood of the traveler because it enhances the acquisition of knowledge, intellect, and communication. Spells with the intentions of art, abundance, and beauty are often cast with Maple wood. It is a perfect wood for healing, purity, and cleansing spells. Hollowed out, it makes a lovely base for incense. It affords you the options for your path instead of having you rely on luck. Magic can be spawn by writing your desires on a special leaf you have picked out and placed in wax paper and sealed with an iron. Make a nice frame and hang it on the wall until the next autumn. Mulched Maple leaves added to your garden will bring successful growth for the coming year. And don't forget the Maple syrup!

OAK

Oaks trees have been around for some 85 million years. Oak is often used for making magically charged tools. Its leaves are used for sacred purification spells and rituals. Placing a sprig of Oak in your car, home, or office can promote prosperity, family unity, and protection. Oak acorns are used commonly for abundance of finances. Burning Oak brings healing and good health, and its ashes, carried in amulets increase fertility, attractiveness, and luck.

It represents a balance of power and can provide strength and wisdom.

Magical Exercises with Oak

- One exercise involves tying two twigs of oak, with red thread, into the shape of a cross and then hanging it wherever you need protection from harm.
- It is thought that if you place a few acorns on a windowsill it will keep away a lightning strike.
- Wearing Oak in an amulet will keep negativity away and bring you creativity.
- On the night of a new moon, plant an acorn and abundance in your life will grow.
- Wear an Oak leaf near your heart and you can avoid being misled.
- Put two acorn caps in some very still water in a bowl and think about a love interest. If the caps pull together, it is a good match, if they drift apart, you may want to reconsider or that the timing may just not be right; you can always check again at a later time.
- Oak Wood fires can magically cleanse illness from a home. If outside it is said that if you catch an oak leaf falling from the tree, you will be safe from flu and colds in the Winter.

PINE

Pine symbolizes longevity because its leaves stay green year-round. Pine magically brings joy and good luck, so you can place pinecones around your home to ward off negativity and gain protection. Immortality, strength in adversity, making it through the tough times, and rebirth are all represented in the mighty Pine tree. The plant's resin is quick to burn and therefore symbolizes the Element Fire. Also, when burning its earthy scent is dispersed corresponding to the Air Element.

Even though the pinecones are considered the tree's womb, they represent masculinity and fertility, sometimes used to tip staves and wands. During Yule they are marvelous decorations in the form of wreaths and branches. Hanging a Pine branch in your welcome area will invite joyous energy and when hung over your bed will protect against illness. Pine branches can be used as a broom to sweep away negative energy out of your home or when placed on your altar will protect your ritual. The earthy scent of pine oil mixed with a bit of water can magically wash away your troubles or any negative entities disturbing you home. Mediating under the magical pine will award you with new perspectives.

ROWEN

Traditionally, the Rowan tree is most sacred, and in Scotland it can only be utilized for only sacred purposes; that means no using its timber or even cutting down the tree unless for ritual. Sacred to Brigid, the Celtic Goddess, Rowan represents, healing, smithing, and benefactor to the arts. Spinning wheels and weaving spindles were made of Rowan traditionally in Ireland and Scotland. Also called the European Ash tree, Rowan trees are actually part of the rose family. Historically, Rowan trees were used to construct ship masts and various handles because of its thick density. It works wonderfully for a carving fashioned walking stick. Ancient ships were adorned with Rowan branches to help them avoid storms, as well as its branches being placed on the doorsteps of homes to ward off lighting. The Rowan tree has also protected the dead from hauntings when planted on the grave.

The magic aspects of the Rowan tree are one of the most sought-after wood species for the construction of wands and staves. Wiccans believe it helps them with their psychic skills and amazingly when the berries are removed from the stick there is the pentacle symbol where they were once attached. Its leaves, dried and ground create incenses magically used to invoke the Elements, Goddess, and spiritual guides, while the leaves are used in spells and love witchcraft. While meditating, Rowan essences help to open the mind and bring you more attuned to nature providing deeper insight as to the human aspect of the universe.

WILLOW

The enchanting Willow enhances magical abilities. It is part of the construction of the Besom. The Besom is usually made from three trees. Twigs of Birch make the broom and functions to rid evil spirits. Ash makes the stave for mystical protection, and the Birch twigs are tied together with Willow because they are most valuable for channeling the energy of the Earth, honoring Water, and locating lost items. The Scottish "Clootie" are springs or wells where strips of rags have been tied to the Willows for the purposes of healing rituals. When a Clootie or prayer rag is tied to the Willow, it is said to release grief. To have a wish come true, ask the Willow permission when tying a prayer rag to its branches. After the fulfillment of your wish, go back to the tree and with a friendly "thank you" untie the knot. In Celtic Tree Astrology, Willow falls on April 15th, to May 12th. It is ruled by the moon and anyone of the Willow sign is said to have many magical aspects of the lunar realm. Creativity, intelligence, and intuitiveness are all characteristics of the Willow sign. To conjure up the Elements and other spirits crush sandalwood and willow together and burn it outdoors at a waning moon. The smoke of burning Willow is thought to guide and sooth the souls of the deceased. It makes for a sacred meeting place for Witches as it wards off evil. It is believed if you knock three times on the trunk of a Willow tree evil will be averted.

YEW

The Yew tree is magically associated with rebirth/reincarnation, protection, and longevity. Referred to by Wiccans as "The Tree of Eternity," Yew wood has great strength. Sitting near a Yew tree is a wonderful way to communicate with your ancestors. Of all of the Earth's beings, the Yew tree is thought of as eternally alive. This is why it is highly valuable to spell works of longevity. The Yew tree lives so long because it can replace its parts anew and so is praised as a tree of rebirth. Many graveyards have Yew trees growing nearby. Some Wiccan practitioners are hesitant to utilize the Yew as its components are poisonous.

MAGICAL USES OF TREES

Type of Tree	Magical Use
Ash	Strength, harmony, skills, water, intellect and protect your home
Birch	Purification, protection, exorcism, cleansing smudge for the house
Cedar	Healing, spirituality, harmony, prosperity, purification, abundance
Elder	Protection, prosperity, sleep, exorcism, protection; must ask Elder tree permission three times
Hawthorn	Fertility, harmony, happiness, faeries, protection, otherworld
Maple	Love, longevity, money
Oak	Strength, fertility, courage, money, longevity
Pine	Immortality, healing, purification, fertility, exorcism, wealth, energy
Rowan	Divination, creativity, psychic powers, transformation, success, divination
Willow	Love, harmony, tranquility, transformation, intuition, healing, growth
Yew	Reincarnation, death, immortality, rebirth

MAGICAL USES OF FLOWERS

Flower	**Magical Uses**
Carnation	Strength, protection, healing
Daffodil	Luck, fertility, protection, love, exorcism
Gardenia	Peace, repelling strife, protection, love, friendship, healing
Hyacinth Iris	Peace of mind, insomnia, love, luck, Prosperity, averts nightmares, grief, pain relief in childbirth
Jasmine	Spiritual love, insomnia, prosperity, prophetic dreams, self-growth, innovation
Lavender	Love, protection, healing, sleep, purification, and peace
Rose	Divine love, friendships, peace, happiness, lasting relationships
Sunflower	Energy, power, protection, wisdom, wishes
Tulip	Love spells, protection, luck
Violet	Creativity, calming effect, prophetic visions, peace, tranquility, protection.

MAGICAL USES OF HERBS

Herbs	Magical Uses
Allspice	Healing, luck, money, energy, determination
Basil	Exorcism, wealth, love, sympathy, and protection, luck.
Cinnamon	Power, luck, Spirituality, healing, protection, love, strength, wealth
Dill	Money, lust, protection, luck
Ginger	Health, success, sexuality, confidence, sensuality, prosperity
Mint	Wealth, healing, energy, communication, vitality
Nutmeg	Prosperity, breaking hexes, bringing luck, protection
Parsley	Fertility, protection, anxiety, money, well-being, vitality, strength, quick recovery from illness.
Sage	Self-purification, grief, wisdom, improved mental ability, healing, spirituality, longevity, healing, wish spells, protection.
Yarrow	Marriage, healing, divination, banishment spells, anxiety, open mindedness

MAGICAL USES OF CRYSTALS AND GEMSTONES

Gemstones	Magical Uses
Agate	Connected Earth Element, matters of the mind, energy, mental health, discovery, truth, stress, depression, loneliness
Amethyst	Connected to the Water Element, Heliotrope, Zodiac Pisces and Aquarius, healing rituals, depression, anxiety, bipolar disorder, stress relief, intuition, cleansing, prevents overindulgence
Bloodstone	Connected to the Fire Element (Mars and Sun), healing, prosperity, fertility, blood health (heart, circulation, menstruation)
Calcite	Connected to the Water Element, Zodiac Taurus, enthusiasm, grounding, healing, joy, mars, money-drawing, moon, purification, success
Diamond	Connected to the Air and Fire elements, fertility, marriage, impotence, intuition, meditation, visions
Emerald	Connected to the Goddess, Taurus, conscious and subconscious, visualization, wealth, love, protection of children.
Fluorite	Connected to the Air and Water elements, Zodiac Pisces and Aquarius, clarity, crystal healing, chakra balancing
Garnet	Connected to the Fire Element, moon magic, menstruation, reproductive disorders, balance, spirituality, intuition, if taken deceptively there will be a curse upon the thief.
Jade	Connected to the Earth Element, truthfulness, serenity, love, innocence, liver, spleen, healing.
Malachite	Connected to the Earth and Water elements, powerful magic, transformation, purification, energy, peace, protection, success, love, warnings
Obsidian	Connected to the Fire Element, volcanos, antitoxin, energy, intuitiveness, subconsciousness, scrying
Pearl	Connected to the Water Element and the Moon, Zodiac Gemini, good and bad luck, protection, prosperity, calmness, spirituality, faith, loyalty, note: if a person believes in bad luck a pearl can certainly bring it because the oyster had to be killed to collect its treasure
Ruby	Connected to the Fire Element, Zodiac Cancer, guard against negativity, creativity, generosity, wisdom,
Sapphire	Connected to the Moon and Saturn, healing, inner peace, spirituality, Zodiac Virgo, intuition, memory, inspiration, protection, grounding, meditation
Tourmaline	Connected to the Water Element, Zodiac Leo, protection from negativity and demons, intuition, spells for self-confidence, personal power, rational thinking, and decision making, promoting a clear view of reality (through illusion and deception) and for spells related to revealing the cause of trouble, or the person at the root of it. Black tourmaline makes a wonderful scrying stone

5

INITIATION TECHNIQUES, FORMS OF WICCA & TYPES OF WITCHES

SOLITARY

Many current Wiccans prefer the solo practice of magic. Sometimes it is because the individual feels they work better alone, and others may want to join a coven but cannot due to family obligations or geographical limitations. Both Solitaries and covens have benefits and if one is not working out, you can always make the change. Some of the Solitary benefits include moving at your own pace, making your own schedule, and not dealing with coven relationship dynamics. The downside is not having someone to share and/or gather your knowledge with. It is not difficult to put your studies aside when learning alone, so it is important to establish a daily routine that helps your move toward achieving your spiritual goals. This may include daily meditations, readings, and performing rituals. Keeping a journal or a Book of Shadows (BOS) of your magical studies allows you to chronicle what has and has not worked for you. Also, by documenting your spellwork, prayers, and rituals, you are laying down the foundation for your own tradition. It is a healthy exercise to look back upon and see how far you have come.

KITCHEN

Magical opportunities arise when taking the time to put together a meal for those you care about. Rather than dumping food out of a can; make it an infusion with magic ritual. Preparing food with your own two hands, lends itself to sacredness and can change the way you think, prepare, and consume a meal; you can practice magic here at the simplest level. The more you become attuned with what life is like to live magically, you may come to notice your kitchen is a magical place. Kitchen Witches commonly have an altar and a stovetop where they prepare their meals. Having a cauldron, candle, and maybe a statue of a hearth goddess can certainly add to the magically inspired ambiance. A display of your tradition including fresh herbs and fresh vegetables are of great importance to the Kitchen Witch. Other practices include keeping the sacred kitchen clean. Physical cleanliness supports spiritual cleanliness. There is no balance in clutter and chaos. Keep on hand your magical recipes in a special book, separate from your Book of Shadows. Consider stirring magic into your dishes with a widdershins (counterclockwise) or deosil (clockwise) direction.

Kitchen Witches use items normally found in the kitchen as magical tools and center themselves spiritually when cooking. Kitchen Witches enjoy using energies from the environment such as essential oils and everyday objects. The Witch infuses his or her own energies into their magical tools to use toward their intentions. They tend not to be overly concerned about a specific recipe and know how to improvise when necessary. Kitchen Witches tend to be passionate about their cooking and delight in trying new recipes and selecting ingredients based on their chemical properties or strictly use their intuitions. Special chants are often used to knead their energy into the final dish.

COSMIC

Cosmic Witches utilize celestial movements and planets in their magical works. Cosmic Witches feel unusually connected to the stars and an increase in their energy levels when working with them. Most Witches use elements of Cosmic Witchcraft as Wiccans honor the moon's cycles and star sign analysis to apply to their spellwork. The difference with the Cosmic Witch is that he or she focuses primarily on celestial events, planets, stars, and even celestial deities. Cosmic Witchcraft takes notice of the planets and stars locations and that allows them to know when and what type of magic can be worked in. Many Cosmic Witches begin with moon magic because it has several phases over the course of each month. Cosmic Witches pick the moon phase that speaks most to them and learn their potentials for use in their life and spellwork. Following placements of the planets and meteor showers are often celebrated by the Cosmic Witch. It is common for the Cosmic Witch to be well versed in tarot, Astrology, fortune telling (tasseomancy) and the study of bones (osteomancy). Many Cosmic Witches listen to celestial music and use it in their spellwork, but mostly for mediation.

GREEN

The Green Witch is known for their healing powers. Green Witches draw power and energy from nature in the form of herbs, stones, oils, gems, and other gifts naturally found on the Earth. Aligning with the name Green Witch is the workings with all things green. It makes sense to the Green Wiccan that if the earth is closely connected to the moon and therefore, the Green Witch tends to focus on lunar cycles. Using crystals, candles, and aromatherapy to support the magic of each moon phase, the Green Witch has everything they need to create a relaxing and rewarding spiritual journey. The Green Witch knows that humans have a strong impact on nature and often make their homes away from the hustle and bustle of city life. They believe you cannot be attuned with nature is surrounded by the noise of a busy life. Sensitive to environmental and animal ethics, the Green Witch senses the rhythms and cycles in nature and can feel the living, dying, and rebirth of all that is nature. The forest is the Green Witches sacred temple.

HEDGE

The Hedge Witch is named so because historically they lived behind the hedgerows along the outskirts of town. Hedge Witches served as healers and used plants and herbs they gathered by the hedgerows in their practice. Hedge witchery involves practices of green witchcraft that is heavily influenced by years of experience, folk customs, and trial and error. Like the Kitchen Witch, Hedge Witches see the kitchen and fireplace as sacred and magical places. Spending a great deal of time practicing herbal magic, the Hedge Witch's practice is deeply spiritual and personal. The Hedge Witch conducts all domestic tasks, whether big or small, from a spiritual perspective. Each meal is created with love and magical energy harnessed from the sacredness of the Earth. Hedge Witchcraft involves dialog with the home in the form of greetings, goodbyes, and a promise to return soon. Pomes, songs, and other gifts are offered to the home opening the Witch's spiritual life to the gifts and protection they have to offer if needed.

AUGURY WITCH

Augury Witchcraft involves interpreting signs in nature. Augury Witches believe that divine spirits live in everything in nature. Augurs interpret and study weather, cloud formations, eclipses, animal behavior, the actions of birds and all other aspects of nature. Similar in practice to a shaman, the Augury Witch analyzes symbols and signs in a person's life, not as a fortune teller, but to find out if the Goddess and God feel that the person is on the right path. They notice any appearances of animals which are sacred to the gods. They are prophetic Witches. In ancient times, Roman priests were called augurs and they interpreted auspices, which means the movement of animals and birds. They also interpreted the importance of lightning and thunder. If the signs fell to the right of the augur it was to be an ill-omen, and those to the east or right side meant a favorable outcome.

Augury Witches start their practice by examining their environment and the wildlife endemic to it. All of the Elements in that environment are important to survival. Flowers and trees are traditional mystic and magical symbols of divination, each with their own characteristics and qualitative. The Augury Witch then becomes oriented to the landscape which is as representative as the animals living there. Looking to the patterns of the terrain and the shape of the land tells the Witch much about themselves. To the Augury Witch, Nature's physical aspects are most important. The three most relevant signs are: the appearance of animals and birds, stones, furs, feathers, and the sounds, chatter, and calls of the animals; where they were heard, and which ones were most noticeable. Paying attention to fragrances and the cawing of birds on one day and sighting a species of tree anew to the Witch are all qualities that reflect an awakening to the Witch's spiritual path. They pay close attention to the colors of the birds, flowers, and energies experienced. Close attention is given to any numbers connected with the animals encountered as then can aid the Augur Witch in where to apply their energy. Notice is taken as to which direction any animals enter their experience, as well as the position (left or right, east or west, north or south), along with how they move in relation to the Witch. During an encounter with an animal, the Witch takes note of the kind of interaction including a lack of interaction. It is necessary to have studied the animal's normal behavior to ascertain the importance of any interaction. Finally, the Augur Witch asks Nature to talk with them by making a conscious action to be aligned with Nature. Sending prayers and thoughts through outdoor mediation asking Mother Nature for communication and signs and then patiently waiting for her answers.

CHARACTERISTICS OF DIRECTION

Direction	*Characteristics of Direction*
North	Abundance, balance, wisdom, knowledge, gentleness, appreciation, intuitiveness
East	Sun Element, rebirth, creativity, newness, healing, willpower
South	Change, transformation, protection, playfulness, trust
West	Visions, travel, dreams, spirituality, compassion, creativity

DRUID

Druid Witches practice magic based on the knowledge from ancient Earth, her stars, herbs, seasons, and primal wisdom. They are all about harmony, reverence, and connection to nature, so many are involved in environmentally friendliness. Druid ritual function to honor prehistoric ancestry. The Druid Witch employs aspects of the Spirit Element to summon protection for nature which is under attack from pollution. Many Druid Witches criticize the mainstream as exploiting the environment and worshiping technology. They feel a sense of belonging to the cosmic. The concept of Awen (Flowing-Spirit) inspires art and poetry. The word "Awen" is chanted aloud three times to involve the Flowing-Spirit, Awen. Awen in Welsh means "inspiration." Rather than covens, Druid groups are referred to as groves because it is a reflection of the trees, which is among the trees the Druids like to gather. Druid ritual is about aligning with the Spirit Element, and generally takes place in the daytime (in the Eye of the Sun). A circle is drawn, and the Wiccans begin hailing to the directions, and then mark out a space where the ritual will take place. Liquid offerings are poured to the ground, and often food items, such as cake, are passed around and taken. Following the consumption, a period of meditation takes place, and an energy from the Earth is visualized.

CONCLUSION

Present day life is one of a fast-paced digital existence which can lead to a total disconnect from your spirituality and from the natural order of things. The aim of this book was to nourish your mind, spirit, and body by incorporating ancient philosophies and practices of one of the oldest religions known to man, Wicca. Wicca is the present-day belief in the union between nature, spirit, and being. It is not only a religion; it is a lifestyle. There are wiccans practicing from every cultural background, every religious background, of every ethnicity and sexual persuasion. Often misrepresented and misunderstood, Wicca is a beautiful way of life that promotes inner peace, a relationship with nature, and healthy ways to foster connections with the Elements and the world within which we live.

While there are many variances between Wicca and other Pagan religions, they share some common philosophies and practices. They both respect and love Nature and want to live harmoniously with the rest of the living and nonliving components in the World. Wiccans honor Nature's phases and cycles of life and death, and many Wiccans personally communicate and develop friendships with many lifeforms, such as plants, animals, and minerals. Rituals are an essential aspect of the Wicca religion, and often are conducted during Full and New Moons, and also at the eight Sabbats (seasonal festivals), which are spread out six weeks apart correlating with the Equinoxes, Solstices, and Cross Quarters (midpoints). Halloween or Samhain in the Wiccan New Year.

By reading this book you have hopefully learned how to practically apply ancient philosophies as a way to harness your inner magic to improve your confidence, happiness, and wellbeing. Frank Bawdoe has shared his in-depth understanding and education of paganism and the Wiccan culture so that the knowledge of how to passionately transform your life through enlightenment and spiritual connectedness is attainable. The Wiccan history was explained to provide a framework for the beginner Witch. Various rituals, spells, and affirmations were outlined so you can incorporate them into your life on a daily basis and create a positive environment to foster inner healing and spiritual growth. Each Element described shows you how to communicate and interpret nature and find strength and solace in the Elements. Natural remedies and healing are a huge component of practicing witchcraft and Wiccans have been doing the research for centuries. The ultimate goal of Wicca for Beginners is to empower you to find spiritual enlightenment, and how to focus and hone your mind to ways you can realize your aspirations while also finding spiritual harmony in all that you do and are.

AUTHOR'S NOTE

I hope you enjoy this book as much as I loved writing it. If you do, it would be wonderful if you could take a short minute and leave a review on Amazon as soon as you can, as your kind feedback is much appreciated and so very important. Thank you.

SOURCES

Akasha & Eran (1996). Gardnerian Wicca: An Introduction. http://bichaunt.org/Gardnerian.html

Cunningham, S. (1988). Wicca: A guide for the solitary practitioner. St. Paul, Minn: Llewellyn Publications.

Gallagher, Eugene V.; Ashcraft, W. Michael (2006). Introduction to new and alternative religions in America. Westport, Conn.: Greenwood Press. p. 178. ISBN 978-0-275-98713-8.

Guiley, R., & Guiley, R. (2008). The encyclopedia of witches, witchcraft, and wicca. New York, NY: Checkmark, an imprint of Infobase Publishing.

Hereditary Witchcraft. (n.d.). The Witch Book: The Encyclopedia of Witchcraft, Wicca, and Neo-paganism. https://encyclopedia2.thefreedictionary.com/Hereditary+Witchcraft

Horned God. (2002). The Witch Book: *The Encyclopedia of Witchcraft, Wicca, and Neo-paganism.* https://encyclopedia2.thefreedictionary.com/Horned+God

Lamond, Frederic (2004). Fifty Years of Wicca. Sutton Mallet, England: Green Magic. p. 63. ISBN 0-9547230-1-5.

Mitchell, Mandy. Hedgewitch Book of Days: Spells, Rituals, and Recipes for the Magical Year. Weiser Books, 2014.

Moura, Ann (2004). Green Witchcraft: Folk Magic, Fairy Lore & Herb Craft. Llewellyn Publications.

Murphy-Hiscock, A. (2009). The Way of the Hedge Witch: Rituals and Spells for Hearth and Home. Provenance Press.

Wigington, P. (2020). "The Rule of Three." *Learn Religions.* learnreligions.com/rule-of-three-2562822.-

Wigington, P. (2020). Eclectic Wicca. *Learn Religions.* learnreligions.com/eclectic-wicca-2562909.

Wright, G. (2015). "Brigid." *Mythopedia*. https://mythopedia.com/celtic-mythology/gods/brigid/.

Wright, Gregory (2020). "Morrigan." *Mythopedia*. https://mythopedia.com/celtic-mythology/gods/morrigan/.

Printed in Great Britain
by Amazon